Love
TOKENS

Love TOKENS

125 ways to indulge your lover

JACQUI RIPLEY

RYLAND
PETERS
& SMALL

LONDON NEW YORK

Senior Designer Toni Kay
Commissioning Editor Annabel Morgan
Picture Research Emily Westlake
Production Hazel Kirkman
Art Director Leslie Harrington
Publishing Director Alison Starling

First published in the United Kingdom
in 2008 by Ryland Peters & Small
20–21 Jockey's Fields
London WC1R 4BW

First published in the United States
in 2008 by Ryland Peters & Small, Inc.
519 Broadway, 5th Floor
New York, NY 10012
www.rylandpeters.com

10 9 8 7 6 5 4 3 2 1

ISBN: 978-1-84597-767-2

Printed in China

contents

Introduction

Love: such a small word for such a powerful emotion. True love is liberating in so many ways. It gives us the courage and strength to be ourselves and to rise to fresh challenges, as well as the confidence to give our heart solely to another. Love helps us become fearless in a world that often seems scary.

So how do you show this emotion other than voicing it? Yes, those three little words are ones we never tire of hearing, but sometimes it's deeds, not words, that reveal our true sentiments. From running her a hot bath after a tough day, to sending him a thinking-of-you card for absolutely no reason, to walking together on the beach barefoot at midnight, this book shows you how to express your love in a multitude of small but significant ways.

Giving your beloved your time, your attention, and your heart will demonstrate over and over again how very special they are to you. This book will inspire you to celebrate your very own love story every single day.

For her

"Love doesn't make the world go round.
Love is what makes the ride worthwhile."

FRANKLIN P. JONES

WHEN she's least expecting it, recite from memory a poem that sums up all your feelings for her.

FIND her to-do list (don't worry, she'll have one!) and write at the end "I will adore you forever" or something personal and totally impractical to make her smile.

CLEAR up your man clutter (you know what it is!) without being asked.

BUY a new book by her favourite author, write a special inscription, and place it by her side of the bed.

NEXT time you're all cuddled up on the sofa together, vanish into the kitchen then bring out a big tub of her favourite ice cream with two spoons.

PICK wild flowers,
arrange them in a
vase, and place it
in your bedroom.

IF she asks, "Does my bum look big in this?" reply, "It will always look gorgeous whatever size it is." She'll love you forever!

BUY a bag of her favourite sweet treats (not chocolates – they'll melt!) and put them in the glove compartment of her car.

SHOP for luxurious scented bath oil. Then offer to run her a bath (this love token will work even better after she's had a hectic day!) and leave the oil in its fancy bottle on the side of the tub to delight and surprise her.

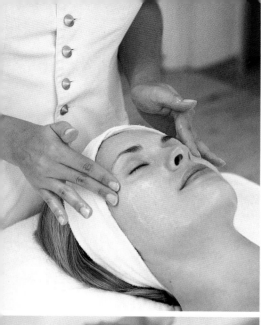

BOOK a pampering day at a spa for her and a girlfriend. Chauffeur them to the spa then pick them up again at the end of the day.

TUCK slushy love notes into her purse and her coat pocket.

INVITE her parents to stay for the weekend. Act like Prince Charming and make them feel like the most wanted in-laws in the land. She will never forget it.

LET her win an
arm wrestle!

DOWNLOAD all her beloved songs (no matter how cheesy they are) onto an iPod or MP3 player. She will value the time it's taken you.

BUY her a designer nail polish and offer to paint her finger- and toenails.

INSTEAD of buying the clichéd set of underwear, do some 'sole' searching instead. Splash out on a pair of to-die-for designer heels. Unwrap them for her, kneel down, and slip them on her feet for the full Cinderella effect.

REMOVE her rubber mat and put a mini sheepskin rug on the driver's side of her car underneath the pedals. The sheepskin will stop her scuffing her high heels!

BUY her a big, soft wool blanket. She can snuggle up in it when you're away to replace your big warm hugs.

SHOW her just how sweet you can be. Ask a bakery to pipe each letter of her name on cute individual cupcakes, then present them to her in a ribbon-tied box.

BRUSH her hair off her face, gently tilt up her chin, look into her eyes and tell her just how much she means to you.

SEARCH out a photograph that means a lot to her, and have it enlarged, mounted, and framed. Her tears will say it all.

BOOK a fabulous holiday. And leave the air tickets or the details of the hotel under her pillow…

BUY her a large, baby-soft, gorgeous cushion. Cuddling up to a luxurious cushion on the couch can't help but take the edge off an exhausting day.

SCRAPE the ice or snow off her windscreen in the morning.

ON a dreary day, lift her spirits by brewing a pot of
fragrant tea and serving it with all the trimmings,
such as mouthwatering biscuits or dainty macaroons.

GIRLS don't always hanker after diamonds.
Find out her birthstone and have the gem
set in a ring or a pendant. It's far more
personal and original.

WHEN it's a frosty morning and there's a chill in the air, get up five minutes before her and place her underwear on the radiator. It will warm her heart.

IF she's feeling a bit down, pin a picture inside her wardrobe door that will make her laugh. It will influence what she wears that day – in a good way!

MAKE her feel incredibly special. All the time. Open doors for her, slip her coat on and off, and never let her sit with her back to the room in a restaurant.

LET 'mum' off the hook, if she is one. Book a babysitter for the night and take her out dancing. Encourage her to really let her hair down.

LEAVE a pair of cashmere socks at the bottom of the bed to keep her toes toasty at night.

GIVE her a beautiful pocket-sized notebook. Look for limited-edition vintage prints, so the book almost looks too gorgeous to write in. Her to-do list will look more inviting and all those boring tasks are more likely to get ticked off.

BECOME a mixologist and do a Tom Cruise impression – shake up a unique cocktail and give it a name that sums up exactly what she means to you.

IF you have a fireplace, summon up your best Boy Scout skills and build a roaring fire. Scatter cushions in front of the hearth, lounge in the light of the flames, and thrill her by toasting marshmallows to enjoy along with a hot toddy.

BUY her a DVD of the modern classic *Bridges of Madison County*, with Clint Eastwood's heart-melting line, "This kind of certainty comes but once in a lifetime."

ORDER her favourite take-out meal, but lift the experience to a whole new level by laying the table and serving dinner restaurant-style. Unfold her napkin, place it on her lap, uncork the wine and pour her a glass. Buy or make a delicious dessert, too. It's the little details that make all the difference.

DON'T interrupt her when she's chatting to a girlfriend on the telephone. Girly catch-ups are sacred! Instead, bring her a glass of wine.

OFFER to join her on her seasonal detox diet.

ENCOURAGE her to go out for the day, then paint the bedroom in her favourite shade. Be handy with the dustsheets so you don't splash paint on any of her treasured possessions!

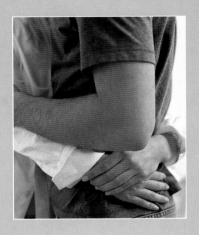

For him

"The more I give to thee the more I have."

WILLIAM SHAKESPEARE

RESERVE one shelf in the living room solely for his CDs. And another for his books. It's easy to shove their 'man stuff' in cupboards, but guys really appreciate it when you make space for them in your home life. It shows you care about both him and his stuff!

PUT your thoughts into words and write a song for him. If you can sing it while strumming on a guitar or piano, even better.

LET him have his 'teenage kicks' by allowing him to play his music loud (occasionally!) without yelling "turn it down!"

WRITE a sexy note in lipstick on the bathroom mirror after he's gone to bed. It will be the first thing he sees when he has his morning shave!

SEND him a romantic thinking-of-you card for absolutely no reason. And post it.

LET him be in charge of the television remote control for the whole night!

DO one of his chores, like mowing the lawn. Chances are he'll do one of yours in return next week.

OFFER to massage his neck and shoulders next time he's hunched over the computer.

SPRITZ your perfume on his pillow when you go away. He'll fall asleep dreaming of you.

PICK up a DVD you know he loves, be it a western, gangster, or action movie, and watch it with him without any yawning or exasperated huffing and puffing.

LEAVE a 'date' message on his voicemail. It could be something like, "I've given the cook the night off (you!) and booked a table at our local restaurant. See you there at eight." It's romantic and spontaneous – what more could a man wish for?

RESERVE a table for high tea in a fancy hotel and invite his mother to join the two of you. He'll appreciate the two most important women in his life sharing time together.

LEARN terms of endearment in a foreign language, then whisper them seductively in his ear just when he's least expecting it!

ORGANIZE a guys' night in for him. Invite a few of his friends around, fill the fridge with beer, switch on the sports channel, then disappear for the evening. The only condition? Any clearing up is definitely his job the next morning!

IF he's going away on business, find out what time he's due to arrive at the hotel. Around that time send him a text saying, "I'm counting the days until I have you back in my arms."

SCIENTISTS have found that men are most aroused by the scent of vanilla. Serve him vanilla ice cream for dessert…

SURPRISE him by throwing off your clothes and hopping into the shower with him. Wash and scrub his back and shampoo his hair for him.

WRITE 10 sentences stating the things you most admire about him. Cut them into strips and tape them around the house.

GO back and buy him something he pointed out in a store window. The knowledge that it registered with you will probably mean more to him than the actual gift.

WHO says men have to buy the flowers? Buy him a bouquet just to show him that the roles can be reversed.

LEAVE lipstick on his collar!

SEEK out the poster of his favourite movie (chances are it's something retro) and have it framed for his cinematic appreciation.

GET up half an hour early and cook him a special breakfast. He will feel spoilt and adored before he even starts his day.

GUYS like being pampered too!
Book him in for a traditional wet
shave using a cut-throat razor
and hot towels. Post-shave, his
face will be baby soft and
incredibly kissable!

BUY him a compass and hand it over with a smoochy note saying he's definitely taken his life in the right direction by being with you!

WASH and polish his car (think of the toning benefits for your arms!). Then give the interior a quick squirt of your perfume. Not too much! You don't want to overdo it…

GIVE him 30 minutes' 'sky-gazing' time when he walks through the door after work. That way you'll be guaranteed a conversation later, not just monosyllabic answers.

LAY his head on your lap while the two of you are watching television, and gently massage his scalp.

DEDICATE a romantic song to him on the radio. Just make sure he's listening when it's played!

IN his glove compartment, place a leather-bound map. You won't be far from his thoughts while he's finding his way around town.

PACK him a gourmet lunch for work. Choose rare cheeses, dark chocolate, and exotic fruit, and place a Polaroid photo of yourself in his lunchbox inscribed with the message, "Happy to be at your service sir!"

WALK and wash his dog, to show him that you're man's best friend too.

FORGET the flannel pyjamas – make it his job to keep
you warm on a cold winter's night by going to bed naked!

PLACE a single red rose on his pillow. It will be the last thing he expects as a nightcap!

WHILE he's engrossed in a film, pour him a cold beer and serve it with popcorn.

❧

CHECK out his Amazon shopping list then order the first three things on it for him. Have the parcel delivered to him, beautifully giftwrapped.

❧

TREAT him to a man-icure. Hold the polish, but go all out on the buffing!

❧

NOTICE when his aftershave is running low and buy him a new bottle. Or take this opportunity to introduce him to a new scent and tell him it's one that sends you wild! Watch him splash and wait…

❧

WHEN he steps out of the shower after a cold and muddy game of football, hand him a thick, cosy towel you've just warmed in the tumble dryer for him.

For us

"Love is friendship set on fire."

JEREMY TAYLOR

MAKE your partner feel like the absolute centre of your universe by hanging on their every word, the way you did when you first met. Ask him or her about their dreams, inspirations, and goals and let your partner talk until they've finished, without interrupting. It's the greatest compliment you can give each other.

PLAY footsie! Kick off your socks and shoes and give each other a long, slow, and sensuous foot rub.

HAVE an impromptu picnic for two. Gather together a few of your favourite foods, a bottle of wine, and a mouthwatering dessert, along with a big blanket, and head for the great outdoors (or even just your back garden!).

PUT on 'your' song, dim the lights (or, even better, light candles), and dance together in the living room after dinner.

SPEND the afternoon having a romantic siesta. There's nothing quite like the pleasurable guilt of having a long, leisurely lunch then heading straight to bed afterwards…

SEE the funny side – enjoy some stand-up comedy together.

WHEN invited to a party, get dressed and make your way there separately. Your mission? To flirt with each other all night long. Chances are you won't leave separately too!

ON holiday, stroll along the beach after dark, barefoot and holding hands.

BOOK a luxurious hotel room for just one night, and don't leave it! Order room service, then make use of the 'Do Not Disturb' sign. Make it a time to talk and enjoy each other in unfamiliar but exciting surroundings.

COOK a big bowl of spaghetti, place it in the middle of the table, and share it.

TEXT each other tantalizing little messages throughout the day. And make sure you carry out your promises when you both get home!

BUY a tree, plant it in your garden, and watch it grow taller, stronger, and more beautiful with each passing year you are together.

JOIN your local gym together. Not only does it introduce an element of friendly competition… but also those who play together, stay together!

FEEL the rhythm. Book a few up-close-and-personal dance lessons, such as ballroom or salsa, to get your toes tapping and your temperatures rising.

ALWAYS give each other a kiss every single day — even if it's on the phone.

ॐ

CATCH a late-night movie… and sit in the back row!

ॐ

ON a balmy summer's evening, make your way hand-in-hand to the top of a nearby hill then watch the sunset together over a glass of wine.

ॐ

THINK of loving things to do for each other each week — such as ironing his shirts or cooking her a favourite meal.

ॐ

RATHER than coming in from a hard day and automatically switching on the television, put on some gentle hip-swaying music. It will instantly put a different spin on your evening by putting you both in a more reflective and upbeat mood.

VISIT a gallery together, then afterwards buy a picture or print that you both love.

ALWAYS put a bottle of champagne (or whatever takes your fancy) in the fridge on a Friday morning. By the evening, it will be chilled to perfection and ready to drink, so you can celebrate the start of your weekend together.

THROW a frivolous house party. There doesn't have to be a reason. There's nothing like making you feel like a loving couple than entertaining your family and friends. Just don't come over as too smug!

REARRANGE the house together. Just like a relationship, a house can become stale if not tended to, which can in turn affect the people living in it. Introduce new textures, colours, and prints and see if it peps you up as a couple too.

KEEP your bedroom sacred. No laptop, no bills, no television, and no phone. Make it all about you two and your relationship, and think of it as your own special retreat.

PAY compliments freely to each other. Even if it's something as simple as, "You smell delicious" or, "That colour looks good on you." Compliments are like little gifts to each other.

BUY the box sets of each other's favourite television series. For her it may be *Sex and the City*, and for him, *The Sopranos*. Then curl up and watch episodes together on alternative nights.

ON a summer's day, hire a rowing boat and moor it on a grassy bank. Lie down side by side, enjoy the warmth of the sun on your face, and allow yourselves to be lulled to sleep by the sound of lapping water.

GO camping, even if it's just for one night. Cuddling up close under canvas is just so romantic!

DON'T be dictated to by time. On the weekend, ditch your watches, boycott the clocks, and just do what comes naturally whenever you feel like doing it.

COVER a kitchen wall with a collection of photos that mean something special to you both. You'll each feel an instant glow of happy contentment every time you look at it.

SHARE everything. Your hopes, your fears, and your dreams... as well as your money and the chores!

GET naked and go skinny-dipping on a warm starlit night!

WRITE 26 ideas each on individual pieces of paper (pick a different colour each). Pop them in a jar then take it in turn to pick one pleasurable chore out each week. It's a whole year full of feelgood surprises!

CARRY out a daily act of random kindness, whether it's bringing him up the paper in bed or lighting tea lights all around the bath for her.

GET in touch with your inner child. Take a day off and go to the zoo, fly kites, or visit the funfair and go on all the scariest rides. Laugh yourself silly and let your spirits run high, just like you did when you were small.

PRAISE more often, and criticize a lot less.

ACT like young lovers. Hold hands, run through the streets, squeeze yourself into a photo booth and pull funny faces while having your photo taken.

BOOK tickets for the theatre and see a romantic play. You can't beat live performances for passion and raw emotion. You may already know how *Romeo and Juliet* ends, but the story never lessens in its passion.

BUY an audio book you both love and listen to it all snuggled up on the sofa one rainy Sunday afternoon.

DREAM up your very own unique anniversaries. Celebrate not only the traditional markers, such as birthdays and weddings, but also the day you moved in together, or the day of your very first date. Surprise each other with an unexpected celebration.

WRITE down everything you love and admire about each other, then swap lists. Sometimes the obvious isn't put into words, but once you've read something you'll never forget it.